ODE TO THE HEART SMALLER THAN A PENCIL ERASER

May Swenson
Poetry Award Series
Volume 17

ODE TO THE HEART SMALLER THAN A PENCIL ERASER

poems
by

Luisa A. Igloria

UTAH STATE UNIVERSITY PRESS
Logan

© 2014 Luisa A. Igloria
Foreword © 2014 Mark Doty

Published by Utah State University Press
An imprint of University Press of Colorado
5589 Arapahoe Avenue, Suite 206C
Boulder, Colorado 80303

 The University Press of Colorado is a proud member of
the Association of American University Presses.

The University Press of Colorado is a cooperative publishing enterprise supported, in part,
by Adams State University, Colorado State University, Fort Lewis College, Metropolitan
State University of Denver, Regis University, University of Colorado, University of
Northern Colorado, Utah State University, and Western State Colorado University.

Manufactured in the United States of America
∞ This paper meets the requirements of the ANSI/NISO Z39.48-1992 (Permanence
of Paper).

Publication credits appear on page 73, which constitutes an extension of this
copyright page.

Cover art by Jennifer Patricia A. Cariño. Used by permission.
Cover series design by Barbara Yale-Read

ISBN 978-0-87421-952-4 (cloth)
ISBN 978-0-87421-968-5 (paper)
ISBN 978-087421-979-1 (ebook)
DOI 10.7330_9780874219791

Library of Congress Cataloging-in-Publication Data

Igloria, Luisa A., 1961–
[Poems. Selections]
Ode to the heart smaller than a pencil eraser: poems / by Luisa A. Igloria.
pages ; cm. — (Poetry award series ; volume 17)
ISBN 978-0-87421-952-4 (cloth) — ISBN 978-0-87421-968-5 (pbk.) — ISBN 978-0-
87421-979-1 (ebook)
I. Title.
PS3553.A686A6 2014
811'.54—dc23

For Ruben

CONTENTS

Foreword by Mark Doty ix

I

Wanderer   3
Derecho Ghazal   4
My Love, I Want to Tell You of Today   5
Dear Epictetus, This is to You Attributed   6
How to Flinch   7
Landscape, with an End and a Beginning   8
Campus Elegy   9
Landscape, with Red Boots and a Branch of Dead Cherry   10
Boy   11
Why Appropriation Is Not Necessarily the Same as Mastery   12
Certified   13
With Feeling   14
Persistent Triolet   15
What You Don't Always See   16
Appetite   17
Letter to Myself, Reading a Letter   18
Intercession   19
Closer   20
Wake   21

II

Mondo Inteirinho   25
Anniversary   26
A Single Falling Note Above   27
Grenadilla   28
Saturday Afternoon at the Y   29
On the Nature of Things   30
Unbelievable Ends   32
In a Hotel Lobby, Near Midnight   34
Landscape, with Cardinal and Earring   35
Empty Ghazal   36
Letter to Providence   37
Letter to Arrhythmia   38
Letter to Levity   39

Interior, with Roman Shades and Lovers   40
Recursive   41
Taxonomies   42
Lover to Lover, Air   43
Imperfect Ode   44
Villanelle of the Red Maple   45
Love Poem with Skull and Candy Valentines   46
Landscape, with Remnants of a Tale   48
Landscape, with Darkness and Hare   49
Not Yet There   50

III

Hum   53
Dumbwaiter   54
Spangled   55
Ghazal: Chimerae   56
I Write Letters to Some Other Sea   57
Improvisations   58
Fata Morgana   60
Aubade   61
Letter to Love   62
Landscape, with Mockingbird and Ripe Figs   63
Mobius   64
What Cannot Eat   65
Landscape, with Sudden Rain, Wet Blooms, and a Van
    Eyck Painting   66
Ode to the Heart Smaller than a Pencil Eraser   67
Unending Lyric   68
Ghazal of the Transcendental   69
Night Heron, Ascending   70
The Wren in the Lilac Cycles through Its Songs at
    Breakneck Speed   71
Reprieve   72
Hallucinatorio   73

Acknowledgments   75
About the Author   76
The May Swenson Poetry Award   77

Luisa A. Igloria frames the fourth poem in this lush, unexpected book with a quote from Epictetus: "*. . . as soon as a thing has been seen, it is carried away, / and another comes in its place.*" The Stoic philosopher may offer this principle as a cause for detachment, but Igloria, I'd hazard, sees things differently: transience, if not exactly cause for celebration, is for her an occasion for the new to present itself. Her poems are drunk with the world's bounty; they fill themselves with life: birds and flowers, Dürer's engravings, tattooed mothers swimming at the Y, fruits whose flavors could hardly be more delicious than their names: carambola, grenadilla, maracuya. The solid ground on which her poems rest is love for the world in all its pungent variety. A goodly part of what I mean by *love* is close attention, a profound interest in and regard for what's out there. Igloria's poetry is a kind of tally, an accounting, a guide to the spectacle of the given, the strangeness and complexity of what surrounds us. *Here,* she seems to say to her readers, I'd like you to look here and here.

But a poem's evocation of reality—that is, a description—must be informed by both feeling and thinking. Human consciousness is a flow of perception, emotion, and ideas about what we think and feel, and a poem often serves as a kind of model of consciousness, inviting us into a version of the poet's subjectivity. This is why poetry is perhaps the most intimate of the arts; it presents the possibility, albeit brief and to some degree illusory, of entering into another person's skin.

Any poem in this accomplished book might serve to illustrate this three-way marriage of perception, emotion and reflection. I'll choose a lovely, characteristically Igloria poem, "Landscape with Sudden Rain, Wet Blooms, and a Van Eyck Painting." The poem is structured by couplets—perhaps to mimic the couple in the Van Eyck, and to underscore the speaker's profound longing to be coupled, herself? The opening lines sketch a painterly landscape:

> Cream and magenta on asphalt, the blooms that ripened
> early on the dogwood now loosened by sudden rain—

The scene immediately provokes a reflection, and not at all one we'd expect:

> Do you know why that couple touch hands in the Van Eyck
> painting?

These dashed blossoms have led, through subterranean associations that won't become clear for a while, to Van Eyck's famous painting, in which a newly married couple pose in their room, between them a convex mirror throwing their image-in-reverse back toward us. The speaker has an answer to her own question:

> Their decorum holds the house pillars up,
>
> plumps the cushions, velvets the drapes for commerce,
> theirs and the world's. See how the mirror repeats
>
> and reflects them back to each other, though crowned
> by a rondel of suffering. In her green robe with its
>
> multitude of gathers, she casts a faint shadow on the bed.

Suffering and shadow: the couple's formal stance, their air of distance and dignity, are read here as a means of containing pain, all that's wrong between them. Then comes a new sentence, one that begins as further description of the painting, but that quickly slides to something else:

> And the fruit on the window sill might be peach,
>
> might be pear, might be apple—something with glimmering
> skin, like the lover and the scar he wore like a badge
>
> to the side of his throat.

The poem has moved elegantly, effortlessly toward its occasion, the disappointment in love that is fueling this examination of both art and landscape. And it is to the landscape of the opening couplet that the poem now turns:

> Fickle nature, cold and grainy
> as the day that spills its seed above the fields, indiscriminate,
>
> so things grow despite themselves. And there was the one
> who said never, but turned from you to rinse his hands.

Spilled seed, what grows despite itself, the one who said never—there's an oblique but nonetheless complete narration of a love affair here, one ending without fruition. And a sly shift has occurred. I read that first "you," back in the poet's question about the Van Eyck portrait, as posed to the reader, or to the world: do *you* know why? But the "you" in that last sentence is clearly the one who's lost in love, a double for the speaker; now we understand that she posed that question to herself, in a moment of discovery, understanding that the painting represented a way of composing oneself in the face of misery. And thus Igloria moves to her sure conclusion:

> Who else loves his own decorum as I do? The names
> of trees are lovely in Latinate. I can't recite those,
>
> can only name their changing colors: flush
> and canary, stripped and rose; or moan like the voice
>
> of a cello in the leaves, imitating human speech.

That artful bit of landscape description we encountered in the first couplet? Now we can understand that was an act of avoidance, of self-distraction. I can name the colors, the speaker tells us, or I can merely moan. Naming "the changing colors" becomes a means both of revealing pain and containing it, just as these decorous couplets provide a kind of orderly structure in which to organize this poem's song of lament. There is the lovely paradox: the poem *is* a moan, but it is a song too. Music is not an outcry, or not only one; it is a made thing that testifies to our persistence, and to a faith in the power and necessity of art. Which sometimes does nothing but make an outcry bearable— but that gesture, in itself, can be quite enough.

Mark Doty

I

WANDERER

O long-awaited, are you nearly here?
Is that your shadow I see from the window,
beginning to cross the field?

Everywhere I look, there are emblems
from years of laboring: nettles
that stung my hands, fronds of palm

braided close to patch the holes
in the roof. Here are shirts
with sleeves of linen to throw

on the shapes of the banished
as they fly under cover of night,
so they too might break free

of their long enchantment. Here
are grains spilled on muddy ground,
where they still shine like pearls

in moonlight: each one now,
accounted for. I read tonight
that certain moths drink the tears

of sleeping birds, *turning sorrow
into sustenance*. O long awaited,
I have never left, I am still here.

DERECHO GHAZAL

And the high winds bore down, and the sky
built up that grey wall: *derecho.*

The taverns by the sea closed their shutters,
and the stands selling battered fries, *derecho.*

On the boardwalk, pieces of salt-water taffy, half-
eaten funnel cakes oozing grease and cream: *derecho.*

And the people on every highway, panicked, sought
a clear route for their exodus: *derecho.*

What's in your emergency backpack? Beef jerky, mineral
water, flashlight, solar cells? Snap in the sound of *derecho.*

Yesterday, white and blue sails pretty on the water;
sharp glint of skyscraper glass. Then this *derecho.*

MY LOVE, I WANT TO TELL YOU OF TODAY:

so ordinary, but so full of portents and disclosures—Please, do not
roll your eyes or sigh, do not accuse me

of having grown soft as evidenced by this surfeit of emotion, as if
hardness were the only worthy standard of anything these days. I tell
you this without unnecessary embellishment,

without premeditation. For once, sit still and let me tell you without
having to think too much about the words—Do you remember the poet

who said that morning, *Why not pluck the ripe fig, why not take the
orange, why not swivel the fleshy globe of the persimmon loose,* just be-
cause it was the brightest

or most immediate thing you saw, the branch bending low over the
neighbor's fence and into your hands? Why not give in to rapture
without comment or accusation, without apology,

resisting the urge to camouflage? And it is the same for every instance
in which a body immolates itself, goes up in a protest of flame and
smoke before falling

off the roof: as in house number 11, Huangshi Village, China, in
April, as a line of excavators stands at the ready to tear the walls of
wood and plaster down, making way for new

grids of steel. *The day dims then spills over into rain;* a current in the
earth crumbles the belfry of an ancient church and the hills bury
children sleeping in their beds—

So it is easy enough to heft moments marked with nothing more
than our ticking silences against such sorrows, and deem them un-
worthy. But something moves again across the field, or passes

the threshold: the smallest movement or disturbance—The mother
soothing the fretful child, the man bending to pick up a creased bill
from the floor.

The one who didn't even know what he had lost, stopped
in the spill of light just before making his way out the door.

DEAR EPICTETUS, THIS IS TO YOU ATTRIBUTED:

Thou art a little soul bearing about a corpse.
And even then you were talking to all of us, weren't you:
ghostly presences in a future we now inhabit, tumbling
swiftly from one gate to another.

Last week, moments before the train departed the Jackson
Street station for O'Hare and a flight I had no idea would be
canceled three times before I could board: a woman got on,
breathless, asking passengers near the doors—

Chinatown? Chinatown? She had on a thin cloth coat,
and her short bob of greying hair was plastered
to her forehead. No one blinked. Perhaps they couldn't hear
from whatever was playing on their earphones, or maybe

they were tourists. Before the doors swung shut
I caught her eye and shook my head, yelled *Red line,*
red line, and she darted off. I don't know if she ever
made it to her destination. *Time is like a river*

made up of the events which happen, and a violent stream:
for as soon as a thing has been seen, it is carried away,
and another comes in its place... Therefore, all that afternoon
into evening, as thin snow began to fall again

on the tarmac, streaking the windows,
chilling the glass, seats filled and emptied,
emptied and filled as though the blue light
flickering near the ceiling of the concourse

were that same river's garment. Anxious passengers
watched as TV monitors showed footage of town after town
hit by a single tornado—New Pekin, Henryville, Marysville,
Chelsea—before it crossed the Ohio River

into Kentucky. The hours stretched, and in their fluid arms
there might have been the call of the mourning dove,
there might have been a sparrow slight as the child borne
aloft before the dark column of air set her down in the field.

HOW TO FLINCH

It's emblematic of our societal discomfort with poetry that so many blurbs for poetry books use the word 'unflinching.'

—Lia Purpura

Yes, I have eaten ants' eggs. Faintly sweet clusters whose honey clicked a little between the teeth. Sometimes, parts of bodies still clinging fiercely by a thread.

The tech on duty explained about the suction created in the vein when pulling back against the plunger of the syringe. *Let me try again*, he said, gently swabbing with alcohol.

Old wives' remedies for warts: drops of muriatic acid. Frog piss. A razor blade cutting clean and across from the base.

Swarms of winged ants—thin waists, bent antennae— after days of heavy rain. Gleam from basins of water on the porch: I cried to see the drowned ones sheathed in their gossamer.

Dear Fyodor, how old will I be when *old grief passes gradually into quiet tender joy*? For hives, sometimes I'm tempted to pass the back of a heated spoon on raised, feverish skin.

In those days, we too looked to the sky
for omens—away from the burning effigies,
the barricades, the soldiers whose phalanxes
we broke with prayers and sandwiches made
by mothers, teachers and nuns passing rosaries
and flasks of water from hand to hand.
The city was a giant ear, listening for news
of the dictator. (Sound travels swift through
a mass of suffering bodies.) Snipers perched
like birds on the peripheries of buildings.
Thickening contrails striped the sky.
Two ravens flew side-by-side over the abandoned
palace, trading hoarse commentary. When night came,
the people scaled the gates. What did they see?
Papers of state whirling in the fireplace. Masses
of ball gowns choking the closet, shoes lined with satin
and pearls; gilt-edged murals above the staircase.
Days and nights of upheaval, their new history
alive; the old one writhing on the floor
with a blur around its mouth like hoarfrost.

CAMPUS ELEGY

If I cried out
who would hear me up there
among the angelic orders?
>   —Rainer Maria Rilke, *Duino Elegies*

We heard the news, we saw on video how
they sat in rows, arms linked, no chorus
sounding anguish from among their ranks.
Or pain, or anger—not that the formality
of silence cannot mean something seethes
beneath the bludgeoned front. Attack the head,
the ribs; pour acids down the throat and
scald the eyes. What civil liberties we take.
A student writes, *They're human too, they hurt*
from all this fear. Long days ahead of vigil;
flushed nights spiked with sudden chill. All's over-
cast. Phalanx of blue: faces that look, as they
close in, like neighbors', brothers', uncles'—
What you see, before the bodies fall to blows.

LANDSCAPE, WITH RED BOOTS AND BRANCH OF DEAD CHERRY

In a photograph, a woman sits on her haunches
amid a sea of debris. Her feet are bare. A pair of red
rain boots caked with mud perches neatly at her side,
the way they might rest in a parlor. Sky the color
of rain, the color of heaving things: water a wall
surging over highways, toppling cars and beams
and lorries. The past tense is already active here—
fields have lost their stenciled borders; there's little left
to read in maps. Above the burning cities, snowflakes
scatter, wandering back and forth like spirits. I watch
one explode against the branch of a dead cherry.
Croak of a raven making the shape of a thousand names.

BOY

Flickering in the light of the neighbor's
surveillance camera, you see this boy

pulling the trash bin away from the curb. He is
thirteen, it is ten in the morning, he is a boy

at home with his mother and brother in a blue
house with a porch and a screen door. This boy

doesn't say anything I can hear, because I am looking
at the last moments of his life on tape: this boy,

from this distance—from beyond frame after frame and from
beyond his life because now he is dead. Around this boy,

what was the quality of the light that morning? Was it
warm or musky like the silk of corn, was it milky? This boy,

and this other boy who walked to the corner convenience store
for a can of soda and a bag of sweets: under his hood, this boy—

And the boy that, surely, once in his life, the white
man brandishing the gun must have been? Only a boy,

each of them. Black face, sepia-tinted body stepping from
shadow into light: how does he become less than a boy?

On camera, two frantic dogs run circles around the man
and the boy; you might hear the voice of the boy

who pleads for his life. Play it again, and still it is the same:
see the man lunge forward, raise his arm, take aim at the boy.

WHY APPROPRIATION IS NOT NECESSARILY THE SAME AS MASTERY

The child wants to know the names of all the herbs and spices on the shelf: those roots floating in a jar like a stunted man treading water, those dried leaves twisted carelessly with twine and left in the kitchen drawer.

Sounds made in a different tongue are often so enchanting—at the start, they are like rain falling, plinking over looped chains in the garden.

Remember that things have names. It is important to know that one thing will not always substitute for another. The beautiful berry leaves a dark stain on the tongue, a body lifeless in its bed.

Remember that a syllable can be slighter than an eyelash. The way it flicks up or down can mean a question, or your chin.

The violinist recounts a fairy tale of a boy kept years with others like him in captivity. They buff the witch's floors to the sheen of glass, gather the fine amber dust in the air to bake into bread, the dewdrops in the hearts of roses to feed her unslakeable thirst.

Later, trying to remember, the one bewitched says phrases over and over. But there is no one there to catch his mistakes, to help him put the pieces back together.

And you, you've been such a good student of that epistemology, of thinking-into-being: don't you know that spells are made of words?

Remember too: not all saying is true.

I have heard another story: how the Pont de l'Archevêché groans with the weight of hundreds of padlocks, etched with promises made to eternity. What happens when the language of the promise is wrong, when the word for "expensive" is used instead of "love?"

Do you glimpse my original shape beneath this overlay of form? The rain falls and falls over the village. The tailor sews in his shop, the fiddler plays a tune by the fire.

Arrival is recognition, which brings a catch in the throat. We weep when words break through a surface. We weep when we have seen ourselves.

CERTIFIED

Here is my passport, my bill of lading, my one-
way ticket, my nowhere fare, my stub you've stamped

to certify. All night I clean the lint
from rusted laundromat machines. All night

I mop and polish schoolroom floors. All summer
while you go off to Florida or France, I tend

your mother's bones, empty her bedpan, feed her baby
food as she babbles in the granny bin. My fingers

have pulled bodies of bitter melon from the vine
and splayed them open on the chopping board.

Come sit and eat with me sometime—I'll make
a meal from seeds and pith, a sustenance of green

and verve plucked raw from my own nerve. I steel
myself, passing through each turnstile, bending

through each furrow, threading the factory needle back
and back into a hundred collars and sleeves—Eyes

that sweepingly appraise the education in my hands,
the dusky sheen of my corn, the perfume of my salt

and pickled shrimp, the bile I drop
into the soup to make me strong.

So what if the beautiful ones always sit in the first row, where the lights strike their hair and jewels the brightest? So what if their fathers have paid for the places they occupy, with little regard for how much it costs others? They post Selfies with captions like "Thing is, I don't give a shit." The potted trees in the atrium are equally beautiful for having no memory of origins. They breathe in the temperature-controlled air but do not bend their branches. A little boy pees in the terra cotta basin, unable to keep it in any longer. Outside, a storm begins its orchestral arrangements: tympani and brass; winds. But night's darkest tuxedo is the mother of all corporations. I want to tell the guard who ushers out the errant boy and his crestfallen parent, *You are mistaken.* It is holy to feel the visceral coursing through you, unstoppable like wind or water. If you ever opened your mouth to the rain, perhaps you might understand how a string stretched as if near breaking gives off that depth of sound. Think of it like stars rushing through the roof. Think of the solitude of the lonely, the destitute, the ailing. Then try to play it again: the kind of music that trembles the skin, escapes the strictures of syntax.

PERSISTENT TRIOLET

We love the things we love for what they are—
the knot's tight fist which fingers coax to feather out,
chipped tooth, false gold, hesitant smile faint beacon from afar;
and yet we love the things we love, difficult for what they are.
Imperfect shape perennially arising from the bath, embarrassed for its scars:
surrender to the ardor that persists, one way or other undeterred by doubt.
This is the way we come to love the things we love for what they are
—the knot's tight fist which fingers coax to feather out.

WHAT YOU DON'T ALWAYS SEE

Now faith is the substance of things hoped for,
the evidence of things not seen.

—Hebrews 11:1

I am the sheen of the egg after it drops its sun
into the heated pan. I am the cool underlining the day.
I am the dry, cracked *bodhi* leaf that falls from the tree

under which the sage closed his eyes and made a perfect
circle with his finger and thumb, and now lies in a frame
bought at the temple gift shop. I am the trill of a cricket

craning its body toward autumn in the heat.
I am the hunger that swerves like a bus on a switchback
trail, so the hens and goats being taken to market

break out of their makeshift cages,
scrambling to safety in the bushes. I am
the tremble in the arc of the pendulum weight

as it hums from the tension of the silver wire.
I am the dream that flickers beneath the eyelids
of the child who wakes then names events

yet to unfold. I am the filament that lodges
in the throat, tasting of salt and bone. And I,
I am the clock that stops just short of despair,

the zipper's train whistling to the end of the track
and back; the shirt that fastens all the way to the top
so fingers can loosen the tiny buttons a little, or a lot.

APPETITE

Mexican Free-tailed Bat (Tadarida brasiliensis)

When the Mexican free-tailed bats fly out
from underneath the Congress Avenue Bridge
in Texas, do they hum the chant of *I want,*
I want as they cut a swath above the capitol,
above the Gaps and Victoria's Secrets
now shut for the night at the open air
malls? Exiting the Bracken Caves
in search of migrating cotton
bollworm moths and mosquitoes,
they'll eat two hundred times their weight
in insects before returning to their roosts.
If only I could feed my hungers in the way
they do, and starve my leathered sorrows
clustering in their caves. So grey and woolly,
they unfurl like a knitted scarf at dusk,
their million eyes like rhinestones
glittering against the cross-hatched sky.

LETTER TO MYSELF, READING A LETTER

Yellowing aerogramme passed from hand
to hand, creases striped with naphthalene dust,

salt-tang over sleepy villages—here's
the broken line of hills, the sweep of coast

caught in a curl of cursive, shadowed
cul-de-sac of consonants bent at elbow

and knee. I'll never know again the knotted
lace of curtains behind which we as children hid,

convinced the sounds behind the heavy doors
were the dead coming to claim our souls.

Here in a sunlit house not my own, I polish
the furniture and floor with oils smelling of fruit

until the heart of the wood is glossy
as an oriole's song, and the rooms

where you come to me again
are a palace of leaves. Summer light,

thick as honey, pooling in squares at our feet:
we ask to be touched, before being taken.

INTERCESSION

Adoro te devote, latens Deitas,
Quae sub his figuris vere latitas...

[I adore you devoutly, O hidden God
truly present under these veils...]
                                        —St. Thomas Aquinas

The silence of falling snow perhaps is like the hush
that lives somewhere in each moment of great
preparation: as for instance in Pieter van der Borcht's
medieval copperplate engraving, when you would not know,
unless you read the captions, that the fierce and terrible
mangled faces of the lion and the lioness are from
their desperate expenditure of chi so that their stillborn
cub might live—under the gnarled cypress and rock,
see how its body writhes, stretching and coming to at last
under the double blowtorch of breath. And what of the meal
that the pelican gathers for her young from the cabinet
of her own breast, bright speckled clusters of blood from
the vine? Feathers fragranced with cedar, the phoenix
bursts into flame then crests from its ashes on the third
day; the unicorn comes to lay its head on the virgin's lap,
and the foliage glistens like a page of illuminated
text. Orpheus knew, afterwards, the dangers of looking
too closely at the silence, of doubting what it might bear.
Think of him ascending from the depths, not hearing
her voice or footfall, not seeing her face. This morning,
also by myself, I bend to attend the furnace's smolder.
Three deer digging under the wild apple tree
in the garden startle and run down the slope.

CLOSER

Closer, says the face to the water—

Closer, says the throat to the song—

Closer, says the spore to the cell—

Closer, says the mouth to the flame—

Closer, says the hare to the hound—

Closer, says the lilac to the unsuspecting chickadees—

Closer, says the leaf to the twig—

Closer, says the *estocada* to the bull—

Closer, says the red heart to the *muelta*
fluttering to the ground in a rain of roses.

WAKE

What remains, what rises early to the surface of the world—Handkerchiefs of snow on cobblestones; overhead, one line written by a jet lost to sight. The eyelash curl of a tilde over the "n" in a name I used to have. Hedges unhooked from the foliage. Brown runnels in the soil. Flamenco music raining little hands of silver from a high window. Flecks of ash on the staircase, disappearing on the sixth floor landing. Palm print on a cafe window. Ink traveling from a page of newsprint to the doorknob, whose muted note of brass gilds your image in reverse.

II

MONDO INTEIRINHO

after Peter Eudenbach

It's beautiful this way, isn't it?
Look at how cobalt swirls define

the snapped green outlines of continents,
the red of territories where cities crackle

with intermittent light or gunfire. Line up
the edges of the clear acrylic cage so they

resemble markings on a turtle shell. Set it
on the shelf, or on an antique roll-top desk

inlaid with gold from melted teeth. Ransoms
have been paid for loveliness less than this.

We've brought war to countless flea-ridden
villages harboring dark wells of oil, beaches

mottled with the dust of diamonds. In return,
see all the trade that journeys back to us

in ochre and blue container vessels, the bills
of lading penned in more than a dozen foreign

tongues. The diners in the inner room
are cataloguing artifacts before their

disappearance: smoked foam of fungi
gathered in thunderstorms, sleek

bodies of eels entombed in blocks
of marbled tofu, ortolans drowned

in Armagnac… For let it not be said
our love is shabby, or lacking for display.

ANNIVERSARY

I too was bent on it, eager to jump
out of the pockmarked skillet and into

the heated cauldron of marriage—*Hurry,*
hurry, said the wind, all the while boring

escape hatches in the tall reeds. *Hurry*
said the lilac, and the jeweled hummingbird

that revved the throttle on its small engine.
Oh, I let them sing their songs of scorching

and I rushed to drink the wine. And oh,
my fingers bled from threading silk

into the needle, from slipping on
my rings of twine. The dish of nectar

tilts from the brittle branches, and the weeds
remain the feathery vagabonds they are . . . Now

I try to learn the gold-slow rhythms of afternoons,
the thrift of hours from the longer bones of time.

A SINGLE FALLING NOTE ABOVE

this chorus of blossoming: some unseen bird,
calling the echo that returns, so each

joy's doubled, brings back its twin—
Whatever name you might give it, whatever
undertone it rings, each bright ripple

shades toward deepening. I used to wonder
what it might feel like, pushed closer
toward the front of the line—place

of dubious honor: the one called on
by whatever might demand a reckoning.
My hair not all completely grey, my hems

not fully rent or frayed; my nerves, my hands
not all quite wrung. I know the days we file
away will not return; this light that pulses

like music in a cage, will go under the velvet
hood. The silver bar inside will swing as gently
even then: its occupant, slight of muscle,

heart large as a sea, will dream of trinkets
thrown into the depths. O, nothing's ever lost,
only unseen, those times the light goes out.

GRENADILLA

Perhaps because I know how salt
is paired with flame and flame's a welt

that licks the skin with thorn and bone,
I've always loved what knows to fold

the piquant tendril in the sweet—
ginger with anise, torn basil with lemon,

the iron bite of bitter gourds lingering
long after summer berries have left

their juice and stain on fingers, lips.
Reptile-skinned melons blush orange

like daylilies at their core, and the moon's
poor copper in exchange. Once, I spooned

a tincture of jasmine flowers and my mouth
transformed into an old cathedral

against whose rose-veined marble walls
sheets of candle smoke lifted, swirled.

Once, I slipped thin slices of the *carambola*
on my love's tongue, so he could understand

how some stars burn greener in their
passing. Shake the purple rind of the *grenadilla*,

the yellow globe of the *maracuyá*—audible pulse,
ticking seeds: exquisite sweet, waiting to explode.

SATURDAY AFTERNOON AT THE Y

The dark-haired woman with the death's head
tattoo wreathed by red roses and flames tosses
her three-year-old into the kiddy pool, and moments
later the child emerges, wildly laughing at the other
end of the lane divider. They do it again. Meanwhile,
I've recognized the man with the slight limp and
one palsied arm who sometimes works at the bakery
cafe, doing water exercises: walking from one side
of the pool to the other. Children are flinging
pink and yellow balls, slapping the chlorinated water
with paddles and foam noodles. All this, of course,
for no reason other than the pleasure of doing so.
Late afternoon sun pours through west-facing windows,
mellower counterpoint to the sauna-like haze
indoors. What did the bluebird mean by saving
his best song for the bluest sky? Or Marcus Aurelius,
who wrote about *How quickly all things disappear,*
in the universe the bodies themselves, but in time
the remembrance of them? When we walk out
of the building, there's light enough still
to make plans for dinner, or a walk, or a movie
at the mall. Everyone has a piece of china
that's never been used, shirts hanging in the closet
with their price tags still attached. The bluebird
should sing instead: Eat from the good white plate
tonight. Dress in your best coat, your purest cotton.

ON THE NATURE OF THINGS

Against other things it is possible to obtain security, but when it comes to death, we humans live in an unwalled city.

—Epicurus

When the radio alarm kicks on at 7:15,
there's an NPR interview with a writer

who's talking about how the world
became modern—Still blurry with sleep,

I listen to a few anecdotes about burning libraries,
then some talk about the Renaissance; and of one

Poggio Bracciolini, secretary to several popes,
who found a copy of Lucretius's *On the Nature*

of Things in a German monastery—which
everyone thought had been all but lost for the last

thousand-plus years. This is the same Lucretius
who wrote about Epicurus, not to be confused

with the website Epicurious ("for people who love
to eat"), where on Thursday the featured recipe

was Turkey Meatballs with Cranberries and Sage.
According to the writer being interviewed,

Lucretius's text (really a paraphrase of Epicurus)
offered readers a view of a world where the most

important human endeavor was the avoidance
of pain. The world itself was made of wobbly

atoms that jiggled and swerved through space,
sometimes colliding with each other to produce

other complex forms of matter, including humans.
In this old-new world, there are no gods, there is

no afterlife, no heaven or hell: and thus the good
philosopher and poet advise that the sager path

is the enjoyment of life and the relishing of its
pleasures. No need to fear death, as when we die,

our atoms will fizz into the ether and our selves,
as we know them now, will vanish. Why not walk

outside to the porch with a coffee mug in hand,
sit in a chair and set your feet upon the railing?

Bring a saucer of buttered toast spread with some
thick-cut marmalade or a trickle of honey, a book,

some poetry. Enjoy the pearly light while it lasts,
and the quiet: before the day and its many

distractions lays siege to whatever little rim
of pleasure you've drawn around this moment.

UNBELIEVABLE ENDS

On the edge of winter, every branch and twig
will soon grow white with rime; and every feeble
plant go under. Not one voice of protest

will we hear when sheets of snow and ice descend,
imperial in their judgment. Which makes me wonder,
in 258 when Emperor Valerian ordered the execution

of the deacon we know as St. Lawrence, what sounds
did the martyr make, roasted alive on a gridiron?
And how far beyond the olive orchards did the smell

of his charred flesh travel? *What end?* asks a famous
poem: choose ice or fire. In most cases, it really
isn't a matter of choice, even when sufficient

will's involved. Take the graceful Isadora, who danced
barefoot, loved improvisation, and led a troupe of
young pupils called Isadorables—she died

of a broken neck when her long silk scarf
caught in the wheel of a car. What I didn't know
was that her two young children drowned in the river

with their nanny, when the French driver forgot
to set the parking brake and the car rolled down
the Boulevard Bordon. I doubt any of them

thought this was curtains, *fini*, the end—
Not even the Kabuki actor who claimed immunity
to puffer-fish poison and asked the fugu chef

for four; or the American statesman who expired
from sticking a piece of whale bone through
his urinary tract to remove a blockage.

Not poor Franz Reichelt, the tailor excited to test
his brilliant invention of an overcoat parachute
(like a cloak with voluminous folds and a hood)

from the first deck of the Tour Eiffel in 1912—
captured on grainy film falling to his death below.
And certainly not the nine people killed in the London

Beer Flood of 1814, when 323,000 imperial gallons
of beer burst out of their vats at the Meux
& Company Brewery. That sudden amber sea,

flecked with foam, gushed into the streets of St.
Giles Parish: destroying homes, knocking down walls,
filling the basements where poor families lived. And they

took the brewery to court, but as in the case of hurricanes
that whirl overhead and ice that hails from the sky,
the jury simply ruled that this was an act of God.

IN A HOTEL LOBBY, NEAR MIDNIGHT

Pick-up Lines

You're 50; I'm 50. So what do you want
to do about it? Even Emerson had cabin
fever. Being in the woods so much,
you'd like just once to feel the mud.
All that walking about, carrying the soul
like glowing embers in buckets. That's
too big a responsibility. And when
something's hot like that, it's better off
meeting something just as hot.
How about we try for some joy?

Response

Correction, I'm not quite 50. And mud is no
big deal, since women have typically more to do
with it than fussing over how their boots have gotten
dirty (have you tried to get it off denim or canvas?)
—Walking, walking, with no destination or design,
no pressing agenda other than reflection: now that's
something I'd like to have the leisure to do. Scribble
in a notebook, pause, scribble again; look up in the trees
where the squirrels run like thoughts as yet unbound;
then come in at no set time to tea, or rum; or more quiet.
As for those glowing embers we carry around in buckets–
I've come to love the way they burn like gathered stems
of willow, like fiery clusters on flame trees: staunch,
insistent, not so easily summed up or dismissed; vivid
hurt against silver-white canes of the ghost bramble.

LANDSCAPE, WITH CARDINAL AND EARRING

The man walking his dog notices that under the bridal
wreath bush, a cardinal flickers like a pilot light.

The woman at her window sees the moon not yet
completely faded in the sky, half a pair of pearl earrings

she still keeps in her drawer though the other
has long gone missing. What parts do we need

to complete each other? Sometimes the day
wobbles like a cart with one wheel.

Sometimes it arrows like a train through
the countryside, even though we don't see it.

We hear its rush onward, its insistent
push toward the distance. The cold

is intense today, and hard to withstand
alone, out in the open. The man gestures

to his dog and retraces his steps.
The woman turns away from the window.

In the bushes, a tiny red brushstroke
wavering in the cross-hatched branches.

EMPTY GHAZAL

Two bright ceramic pots beneath the window: purple for starbursts
that haven't seeded, orange for lavender. In other words, they're empty.

Waiting at the doctor's, a feathered strip glimpsed beneath
the awning. Blue wing, black bars, then the space emptied.

Geckos call on the fringes of the factory where young migrant workers
cobble computer tablet parts together. The suicide nets tonight are empty.

There are days I want to move boxes out of cold storage, not
knowing what's inside: take them to the curb; purge, empty.

Cleaning my drawers, I find a small stack of unused journals.
The leather-covered one you gave me, my favorite, is still empty.

I dream of choosing a rich Japanese ink to fill my pens, with names
like Dew on Pine Tree (Syo-Ro) or Old Man Winter (Fuyu-syogun).

How much a flourish on cream stock gathers: scroll of morning glory,
blush of persimmon. Wildness of horses' manes, the horizon empty.

Loosely held, the brush gathers the line as it goes. Uncertain at
first, it stumbles on the trail, then speeds: moving away from empty.

LETTER TO PROVIDENCE

Dear hidden estate of which surely I
am queen, what is your weight in stone,
in paper, in gold? I hold your promises
carefully in one hand while with the other
I wield a rusty machete to clear a trail
through underbrush, through screens
of twigs and bramble, turning logs and small
boulders aside. You've always been a few
nimble steps ahead—sometimes disappearing,
then beckoning with a quick flick of the wrist,
a hand-lettered sign spelling *Home*.
And who would not hunger for such a vision:
an acre, a hollow, a nest no matter how
small, no matter it weighs as much
as the bird that built it. . . . Be legible
now for me, convey such simple trust:
that willingness to indemnify my
years of hard wandering, at last.

LETTER TO ARRHYTHMIA

Dear arrhythmia, dear perennially
sidestepping, asynchronous and rapid
tachycardia, I've learned not so much
to fancy up my footwork as to fake
a passable improv: not even time
to do my nails, check my hair or lines
for an audition call—but here we are
again in the molasses of a telenovela,
gliding from moments of near hysteria
then shimmying to the Copacobana
as doors revolve like windmills
in the background. . . And it's true, then,
what they say about you: how you break
knees, break hearts, and then ask
Will you dance? Sometimes I want to stop,
just be the wallflower, enjoy the view—be
the one the waiters come and tend to,
their silver trays bobbing with fancy,
pileated tufts of napkins. Oh but I've never
known the ease of a downier partner:
only you dealing and dealing it out;
sometimes, more than I can muster.

LETTER TO LEVITY

Dear buoyancy, dear levity, dear
little digression; dear necessary respite
from gravity and circumspection, your voice is
just audible over the wind like a junco's chitter—
Leaves like tongues lift from the newly melted
forest floor, busily trading all kinds of news
from the world—for instance, why did I not know
before today of Qaddafi's all-girl coterie of virgin
bodyguards, smart as models in their khaki outfits;
or of how he sometimes likes to camp out in five-
star hotel gardens in a sumptuous, heated Bedouin
tent guarded by a camel? Or of Unsinkable Molly B,
the cow that jumped a slaughterhouse gate and fled
authorities by swimming across the Missouri river?
(She's safe now in a Montana sanctuary.) They say
that Elton John's in town this weekend: I want to know
if he's traveled with the same grand piano that workers
in Tsarkoye Selo scratched their heads over, wondering
how to hoist it through the narrow windows of Catherine
the Great's gilded ballroom. And what about those three
men in Malaysia who made off with 725,000 condoms
(still missing), or the Mexican woman now on her ninth
day of a hunger strike, demanding an invitation to Prince
William's wedding? A 35-year-old naked man was captured
on surveillance video taking sausages from the kitchen
of a retirement home. Who knows why these things happen?
Perhaps an inexplicable longing seized them all in the night,
some order not to be disobeyed flashed on in the cortex
of the brain. Once, my daughter's piano teacher mistook
a gift of strawberry body butter for yogurt. She called,
half laughing and half in pain, saying she was just
so hungry, that it smelled so beautiful and good; and
suddenly she wanted it, more than anything in the world.

Do you remember I told you about the afternoon
in the coffee shop, the heat another layer of white
laid across the stucco, the silver samovars lined up
on the shelf next to blue and yellow ceramic bowls,
the espresso machine hissing in the corner?
Distracted by so much warmth, I asked the girl
tending the register if I could draw the sheer
Roman shades partway down. And then
the man walked in, mobile phone at his ear,
hips sheathed in denim; white shirt off-setting
a burnished face, the grey hair at his temples.
He carried a gift bag swathed in ribbons. Outside,
tiger and spicebush swallowtails splayed open
their wings, circled, then rested on the white lilac.
The woman he was waiting for arrived.
They took the table farthest from the windows.
They held hands, they kissed. *Birthday?*
smiled the girl bringing cappuccinos and napkins.
The woman smoothed her dark brown hair.
Packing up my papers and my books and pens,
I peered at the sky. If it had rained right then
I might have gone out under the trees to be
like the lover and his lover, awash in that murmur
passing like a single flower between them.

RECURSIVE

Do not look for illumination.
Mostly there is the twitch that precedes
gesture, the button's resistance
as you try to slide it into the too-small

aperture slashed in a finger-width
of cloth. And yes, I know it is hard to disregard
how tiny and even the stitches are,
how they ring the space

that had to be opened first
to make way for the fastening.
Don't feel betrayed
if there is only silence

in the trees, months of near
continuous rain. Thoughts sometimes rush
to collect at the bottom of the drain pipe.
Other times they vaporize in the heat,

fall for the voices warbling discontent.
When it rains, I am oddly comforted.
The rain soaks through, asks me to give up
a little of myself. Asks me not to be so hard.

TAXONOMIES

At low tide, the women
set out folding chairs on the sandbar
and read, their hips half in, half out of water.

*

Across the channel, a line of birds
on the distant rocks—The pelicans leave
first when our boat approaches.

*

All night, the lamps beneath
the hotel window turn curtain panels
into rippled furrows.

*

Streets named after fruit and flower
and tree. Salt marsh snails and periwinkles
on the floor of the bay.

*

Bricks in the wall where a vault used to be.
High ceilings studded with metal arches.
Rice grains in the salt shaker.

*

We are told to follow the gravel road
to the end of the harbor. To get to where
the water ends, we cross a rusted train track.

*

At dusk, the sky looks windswept, nearly
empty. Only in the mind, for now,
somewhere, rain is falling.

LOVER TO LOVER, AIR

to eagle, bell to bell

in the great carillon
where one sound

silvers and multiplies
into a choir of tongues:

at the end, make me tender
from having lived the lessons;

give back the frayed
untangled, return

me to myself
just as the measure

loops firmly back
into itself.

IMPERFECT ODE

Give thanks for the wobble of the wheel
and the limp of the pulley, the tiny pop
in the heart of a light bulb as it goes out—

Give thanks for the pause that loosens the noose
around the rushing hours, for serifs of rain
trickling down the blue gradations of a chain—

And give thanks for the call of a dove
that has lost its mate, and so tinges
your day with the blue of this reminder—

Forgive the stumble of the bow across the strings,
the hair of one note that flies away from the score:
give thanks for our common imperfection.

VILLANELLE OF THE RED MAPLE

Like a question surfacing in the mind of winter,
at last the red maple blossoms are open.
Rich red anthers, puffs of orange pollen—

they are why the white-throated sparrow sings without
stopping in the rain. How does such love happen
like a question surfacing in the mind of winter?

I trail my hand in shallow water, and dredge up
questions no one can answer. I have no weapon
against the richness of red, the puffs of orange pollen.

The lover asks, *What need for questions,*
when the soul has met its answer? Fire might dampen,
doubt flicker in the mind's unfinished winter.

The bird sings its pure white carol in the leaves,
singing, singing—as if the heart knew no other burden,
only the richness of red, the tenderness of orange pollen.

I let it sing, I let you come to me as you have all these years.
I had been tired, I had been lonely. I wanted to open
like a question meeting its answer at the end of winter:
heart rich with red, its joys stippled like puffs of orange pollen.

LOVE POEM WITH SKULL AND CANDY VALENTINES

And everich of hem did his besy cure
Benygnely to chese or for to take,
By hir acord, his formel or his make.

—Geoffrey Chaucer, "Parlement of Foules"

Cosmedin, Rome: in the Chiesa di Santa Maria,
a flower-wreathed skull sits preserved in a shrine
more ornate than any foil-covered box of candy—
that's Saint Valentine himself, as the hand-lettered
strip of bandage across his brow proclaims.
"Protector of love," martyr of Terni, he got
couples hitched at a time when—would you believe—
it was illegal to marry. The stories say he was *beaten*
with clubs and stoned; and when that failed to kill him,
he was beheaded outside the Porta del Popolo.
Poor Val, his aquiline nose may have been broken.
But he seems to have kept most of his teeth, which rest
(some gaps between, though they say that can be sexy)
just inside the edge of the reliquary frame. His gold box
resembles a 1930s RCA TV, or the consoles in the *Doctor*
Who episode where an alien disguised as a woman is trying
to take over the world. Even here, the theme is love
and monsters; or love and sex, lust, appetite, desire—
everything you want but can't actually have, so naturally
you want it even more. On the eve of the festival
of Lupercalia, young Roman boys and girls wrote
their names on slips of paper and put them into jars;
then they held a grand old raffle to find out who
they'd walk hand in hand with the next day, share
a honeyed sweetmeat with, maybe spoon a little,
golden in the olive grove. Did the trees make noise
under the cloudless sky, touching in ways we
rarely do? Everyone loves a little sugar every
now and then; why not them too? Cushioned
in red and gold, the saint would understand
the meanings of excess: candygrams and chalky

conversation hearts (*Sweet Dreams, URDGR8ST,*
Be Mine, Big Hugs), little mounds of milk
chocolate goopy in their maraschino centers,
cardboard boxes lettered with their swirly
tic-tac-toe of X's and O's; lacy thong, slinky
sarong, velvet codpiece. Welt of pepper and spice,
ascetic stripe of sea-salt on the hungry tongue.

Like them, we were young once at the bend of the road where the trail enters the woods. No one who goes in emerges unchanged. Watch the way the colors shift on the bark of trees, from russet to carbon, to old serpentine. We turned the stones over, lay our bodies across their moss. Who cared what the sunlight touched? The littlest stones looked glazed with sugar. Feathers flashed in our hair—stippled, brilliant with color, purple and green. Egged on by hunger and need, our tongues were quicker than quick. It was always now or never; always fire, fucking, curses. Our hearts never stopped banging at the door. And then, the tollways reached, the fumbling for ivory card stock embossed with names. Under the moon, on the winding trail, our pockets rich with crumbs.

LANDSCAPE, WITH DARKNESS AND HARE

There are still some places on this earth
where, driving into the hills just ten miles
from the nearest town, if you killed
the engine and turned off the headlights
you would find yourself at the bottom
of a well of darkness. Perhaps it is too late
or you don't realize I hadn't planned
on coming this far down the road,
but here we are. We could have taken
the other exit, the one littered with rest
stops, vending machines dispensing packets
of sugared goods all day and night, glass
vaults offering the sliver of a chance to lift
a cheap stuffed animal out of the felted pile--
But whether or not you really meant to sign
on for this ride, we're too far inland now.
Cell phone signals come through only
intermittently, and on this stretch the houses
are three or four miles apart. Who'll break
the silence first? Back there, I saw a painted shingle
that said to watch for deer crossing. Even in this
desolation, so many signs of life, as though they
didn't require our noticing. If we sat here
through the last icy hours of night, we might see
at first light, juncos on the snow between
the cattails. Or Dürer's young hare, soft brown
in watercolor and gouache, still for a moment
before disappearing in the grass.
With all my heart oh how I wish he
would take all the darkness with him.

NOT YET THERE

The tree is intricate, a lattice
with many moving parts: sparrows,
robins, a blackbird's creak.

The ox in the sky pulls the plow.
The archer strings his one good
arrow across the bow. The dipper's

hinged against the lip of the grassy well.
And I have only my hungry heart, my
wobbly heart: I cart it everywhere I go.

III

HUM

In the high grass that rippled like a sea, we played at finding, hid-
ing, disappearing. In and out of the shadows, the sun flickered like
a lazy fish, a silken flag, a golden eye whose tears spooled thin into
a bowstring. Straight down we slid, and down again, to where the
ground dipped like presentiment of treachery to court that sharp fris-
son of danger: rocks to tatter our clothes, any abrupt edge to catapult
us through the humid air—We touched and tasted salt of our sweat,
whelped cries from our furious labor to break through circles that
ringed our homes: bees in their hive, the honey-fat queen glued fast
in her cell. All the drones circling and circling, sentinels divested of
their sting.

DUMBWAITER

Around the table, they spoke
of their great accomplishments
and honors—A woman fished
a string of beads out of her jeans
pocket and pointed to each in turn,
naming the taverns and bars
where she'd stumbled onto the stage,
microphone or no, to read her verse.
One whispered there were at least half
a dozen moist narratives growing in his crotch
and armpits; he was merely their vessel,
obedient slave. Another combed and plaited
her muscular hair with a clutch of long dashes.
All night they ate platters of words
served out of season; all night they drank
of what was freely appropriated, wines
forced from fruit not certain of their vintage.
When they copulated and gave birth to offspring,
they were so moved by the originality of this
achievement that new industries were built
around their need to find footwear
or skins of leather equal to or greater in value
than their own flesh and blood. But there were others
who walked among them filling glasses, folding linen,
answering the summons of a buzzer laid in the floor
beneath the dining table, dusting the long-untuned
grand piano, the books unread in the library.
There were others who relished the dusk
and the solitude it delivered, the quiet
like a seed one is tempted take in the mouth
in order to stay elsewhere, underground.

SPANGLED

You think you know but you don't know
shit about what we've been through—

You think we got here only yesterday, but we jumped ship
long before that voyage and landed in the bayou.

You think our backs would break from counting beans,
harvesting fruit before our fingers grazed first dew.

You think below the deck, on KP duty, meant to shine
the captain's shoes: but never rising in rank, in the crew.

You think fling, short time, good time, Johnny come
quick and gone. Cheap roll in the hay? Screw you—I don't do.

You think old school, passé, uncool. I beg your pardon:
above your designer waistband, your butt crack shows in review.

You think the fireworks spread their veils of weeping willow
just for you? World upon world of the wounded: their histories accrue.

GHAZAL: CHIMERAE

First poem, last poem—Confession: I'm always writing
that dream book, wandering with its chimeras.

Wind and fog, and then just wind. Silhouettes of goldfinches
indistinguishable from leaves. Then silence like a caesura.

In the *Iliad:* a thing of immortal make, not human, lion-fronted,
snake behind; goat in the middle, breath from a hot caldera.

Always I'm of more than two minds: heart ravenous as a craw,
mud-burdened as an ox. My real self, vertiginous in the sierras.

It's late November and birds come back in droves to Mt. Ampacao.
In darkness, hunters wait: 20 meters of nylon nets strung along the *frontera*.

From high up, the flush of bonfires must look like dawn; terraces,
low stone walls against the mountainside, like streaks of dark mascara.

High-pitched cries, feathered bodies in the mesh. I'm not there but I
too pan the air: I want what flies, what lifts my pulleys, bones, my aura.

I WRITE LETTERS TO SOME OTHER SEA:

to the hornbill sending its call
along the bluffs, to the wide-eyed
tarsier clinging to the end
of its branch—There, too,
the moon is round as a paper
lantern, the waters dark
blue and seeded with dreams.

IMPROVISATIONS

1

Hail raining down on lake water means I have hurt you.

Translation: The burn that makes no noise,
the scarlet inflorescence of the skin.
The moon's neon sign reads smolder. Why
do you think you hear fire sirens in the valley?
But you don't move, you stay.

2

And the leaf was no longer a leaf but a trellis of itself.

Translation: Coming back from a walk
in the woods he spoke of a ribbon of floating green;
of how, going closer, he saw the near-invisible
spider silk, its tether to the canopy. Say lace,
say beautiful flayed skin.

3

Light is always liminal.

Translation: Spittlebug striped cinnabar and clove,
frothy beard caught in the hollows. Nearby
is beebalm, nearby is sage. Such overdrawn
tenderness we cannot help. We finger each
slick bubble, think we hear the tiny pop.

4

The clouds are sheets of cotton pulled thin between our fingers.

Translation: At the lake, villagers are harvesting
shoals of tiny fish, their bodies an inch long, the dark
pupils of their eyes no bigger than pinpricks.
The water ripples like oil.

5

*You lean forward and say, Don't move. There is an animal in the tree
above you.*

Translation: The nuns in the school I attended
made us walk, single file, up and down the narrow
wooden staircases: Only on the balls
of your feet, girls, they commanded.
Lightness is all.

6

*Where can I go to feel sand under my feet, watch the rush of water tint
them sable?*

Translation: The Japanese irises wear thin
wrappers of color; they've had too much heat
and now they're shriveling in the evening air.
A cricket twangs its strings in the shadows,
oblivious to the deep vermilion pouring over
the harbor. Not me—I want to drink it up.

FATA MORGANA

What is the name of that goddess in the print, her arms full of instruments for music and torture, her mouth beautiful like a flower or the tip of a spear, her red-painted feet flashing across hot coals and a circle of fire? I am not cunning like that, I am not fierce or graceful, and it's become harder to read more than one book at once. Do you remember when I tried to cook two things at the same time on the two hot plates of the stove? One saucepan was burned so badly we had to throw it away. And as I stood in the yard before I dropped the piece of disfigured metal with its melted plastic handle into the trash, I remembered the way my father looked just hours after his death, laid out on a bed for want of a coffin, arms folded on his chest in the attitude of peaceful sleeping. His skin had not cooled yet, his cheeks had not taken on the hue of those who've started walking away from this place and will no longer look at the spill of late flowering blooms by the fence. With my two arms I hugged myself the way another would. With my two hands I gathered up and tied my hair, I walked back to my house of appetites, my house of things, my life of many parts waiting to be wound and folded, mended, counted, found.

AUBADE

The pressure of a wheel turning on soft gravel,
a window sliding open. What sound is made

when something slips away and the hand closes
and opens on nothing but cool air in its wake?

The man stirs in the dark and sees the fog
caught in the treetops, the water beyond

just beginning to catch the light as it rises.
He's restless, or he's preoccupied with worry.

It begins to rain but he takes his bike
out of the garage, thinking he might follow

the distant chirping of quarry trucks to their source.
It's early, and even the dog won't go. Too early

for the dog; it won't go, but watches him
pedal away in the rain to try to trace the sounds

that roused him, back to their source—not birdsong
though a restless wingbeat rises in the air, and the light

begins to catch at the edges of water. It passes
like fog through the treetops, through his hair;

it passes like a hand closing and opening. That's
the heart missing what it wants to hold fast.

Look out the window—flicker of narrow
tires on the road; rain, soft earth, loose stones.

LETTER TO LOVE

Dear fellow wanderer, familiar now as my twin,
more handsome than my shadow: all these years
we've stopped at the same wayside inn to share
quick meals, a cup of coffee, talk about our days
and where we've been—And yet we never linger
longer than an hour, perhaps two, before the claims
of the world descend again. But now I don't know
which is more magnetic: that tilt of sky, the road,
plain countryside rampant with scent, tall grass
where the wind could lift our names higher.
Memory or dream, was that your kiss under my
eyelid's flicker? I miss you even before you've taken
leave. This morning is full of the cries of woodpeckers—
part ululation, part rusty hinge. Your heart goes
with them, or forages among the stones with sparrows,
trusting in what it finds. You never say *So long*
or *Au revoir*, only *Next time will be sweeter.*

LANDSCAPE, WITH MOCKINGBIRD AND RIPE FIGS

Like a wren, like an oriole, like the quail—
there's the mockingbird improvising in the grass.
Chittering call of a Cooper's hawk, jay that calls
and calls until his double answers. Who
hears my voice crying out in the middle of the day,
who knows to tell the echo from its answer?
The Japanese beetles have gored open
the sides of figs velveting the tree.
You picked my hair clean of shadows.
You dropped little stones in the beaker
so the water rose and I could drink.
Sweet smell of clover, sweet-fingered fruit
ripening to rot upon the sill.
Above the sheets, a spider couples
with its prey. In their eyes' prismed glass,
our limbs bond into brittle sugar.
That isn't steam beneath the ceiling.
Outside, small birds continue feeding.
A strangled cry. Finally, the jay calls like a jay.

MOBIUS

The flower dangles by its stem; the stair-
case peels its progress, plank by plank,

diminishing into that well of light
we call *a landing*: what shore suspends

midway between the gradual earth,
the gradual sky? Night turns to day,

and day to night, reversing strip that
lightens at the edges. Lovers meet

and then soon part: whispers in the hedge,
while in the air, haloed and beaten,

disc that floats like labor's emblem, its
coat-of-arms. Burnished and driven, I lip

the rain that poems the smallest flame,
that dangles the flower from its stem.

WHAT CANNOT EAT

How long does hunger hold? Or joy
forestalled? I know that hunger climbs

the trunk of the tree, persistent at its task.
If only each open cup, each well

of blossom had drink enough to douse
that flame—If only the moth that scrolled

its richly tattered cape across
the bark had a mouth; if only its four

half-moons were radiant feast,
enough to settle my restless songs.

LANDSCAPE WITH SUDDEN RAIN, WET BLOOMS, AND A VAN EYCK PAINTING

Cream and magenta on asphalt, the blooms that ripened
early on the dogwood now loosened by sudden rain—

Do you know why the couple touch hands in the Van Eyck
painting? Their decorum holds the house pillars up,

plumps the cushions, velvets the drapes for commerce,
theirs and the world's. See how the mirror repeats

and reflects them back to each other, though crowned
by a rondel of suffering. In her green robe with its

multitude of gathers, she casts a faint shadow on the bed.
And the fruit on the windowsill might be peach,

might be pear, might be apple—something with glimmering
skin, like the lover and the scar he wore like a badge

to the side of his throat. Fickle nature, cold and grainy
as the day that spills its seed above the fields, indiscriminate,

so things grow despite themselves. And there was the one
who said never, but turned from you to rinse his hands.

Who else loves his own decorum as I do? The names
of trees are lovely in Latinate. I can't recite those,

can only list their changing colors: flush
and canary, stripped and rose; or moan like the voice

of a cello in the leaves, imitating human speech.

ODE TO THE HEART SMALLER THAN A PENCIL ERASER

after Brian Doyle's Joyas Voladoras

I don't know whose translucent wings those are
twitching, disappearing into a knothole in the ceiling;

but in the throes of great uncertainty I am
asked to consider the miniature:

* A heart the size of a pencil eraser, beating ten
   times a second, hammering faster than we could hear.

* A heart that fuels flights more than five
   hundred miles without stopping to rest.

* Hot heart that kisses at least a thousand flowers a day
   but cold, slides into a torpor from which it might no longer rouse.

* Oh my constellation of fears, shamed by a wingstroke
   smaller than a baby's fingernail, thunderous as the world's wild waterfalls.

* Heart like a race car engined by color, buffered
   by wind, stripped for nothing but flight.

* Chant of bearded helmetcrests and booted racket-tails,
   violet-tailed sylphs and crimson topazes.

* Rosary of charismatic names: amethyst woodstars and
   rainbow-bearded thornbills, pufflegs and spatuletails.

* You've found me out: I have a bag of tortoise coins. I've spent them
   like a miser, hoarding each little bit of copper against that one stupendous day.

* I've lived mostly alone in the bricked-up house of my heart,
   but a wind teeters at the door, all skin and apple breath.

Zealous at long rehearsals, tenacious at audition—the brushed
yellow-olive, drab-coated vireo hangs upside down then
exits the tree with a prize: red berry or dun kernel, blur of
winged insect disappearing down the hatch of its throat.
Valediction isn't its song: not a saying farewell, not the
up-swelling notes of a soprano—just the same
tremulous question and answer all through the day.
Sound shivers like a string when plucked. I learned
rote-singing, then followed the pencil across the staff:
quarter-notes, eighths, sixteenths; the rests like little
puffs of breath propelling onward. And yes it's work,
opening the chest to let the air of longing out for that
nimbus of release, though brief and incommensurate.
My audible heart wants a nest like a cup in the fork of a tree.
Lit up at night, in that forest of softened trills, who
knows how the air might shear its stuttering refrains,
join the failed parts of songs as leitmotif?
I practice and practice though nobody hears.
Hoarse from effort and nearly at empty, I
gloss sometimes over difficult parts that
find a way of coming back, sliding into another
edge of passage. Nothing ever stays still:
do you see how the moon shimmers, then
clears a path for the screech owl's call?
Bright, brassy, or somber rounding in the mouth—
answer that burns salt shapes on the tongue.

GHAZAL OF THE TRANSCENDENTAL

Why can't the Buddha vacuum underneath the sofa?
Because he has no attachments.

—Kaspalita Thompson

One of the neighbors has a new statue of the Buddha, plunked down in her garden.
Perhaps she got it at a Black Friday sale, camped out all night, came home singing.

The Buddha teaches that we want to work free of delusion and suffering
in order to ascend, like the wren in the lilac, full-throated, singing.

I don't know too many intimate details about his life but I do know
the Buddha was not a woman doing chores all day, much less singing.

Suffering is a pain in the ass, in the neck, in the heart mostly; since I
suffer knowing my children's hurts, will I never know that lithe, joyous singing?

So the sacred verses speak of attachment and illusion. I know, but with all due
respect, it's hard to feel detached when you nick yourself shaving (not singing).

Perhaps in the wilderness, in solitude, there might not be the struggle that comes of
engagement:
but even then, there is the noise the mind makes in its own singing.

The Buddha can't vacuum underneath my sofa. Or under the beds. Or do the dishes.
I know, I know. If I were to detach from these tasks, they'd be easy as singing.

And one must sing rather than drone, don't you think? Even in the bramble, that's
what the birds are saying: the richer the song, the more complex the singing.

NIGHT HERON, ASCENDING

Through the window by my desk, I see a poem light in the branches
of a tree. It roosts awhile, then leaves—Night heron, ascending.

My friend thinks it an omen for something good and rare. I regard the question
mark of its neck and back, its feathered cap streaked with pale saffron, ascending.

Last season's big storm flung a nest with young herons to the ground.
Perhaps this is one of them, out of the rhododendrons ascending.

In *The Conference of The Birds*, what fate befalls it as the flock undertakes
the journey? A blur past oak, ash, and willow; past reddened crags, ascending.

From that height, boats are specks on the water, and we, even smaller.
Which dark craft at the river's mouth is Charon's, swiftly descending?

In this summer light, some things look struck by gold: mythic, emblematic.
Portentous spirit, wings outlined with neon—tell me of ascending.

THE WREN IN THE LILAC CYCLES THROUGH ITS SONGS AT BREAKNECK SPEED—

And why not sing? And why not burn a track
from the tinder of the branch to the furnace of noon?

The maw of that which will devour us all,
that gapes beyond apartments and old strip malls;
the rusted iron gates over which the neighbor's ivy creeps,

unpeopled mansions built
on mountaintops exposed, tracts of sand
over which armies of boots grind children's bones

to dust—And why not empty
all the vessels of the throat,
the glittering receptacles of blood;

and why not break
the hundred glasses in the room
with the sharpest facets of that joy,

that long-lost twin of sorrow?
Hurry through one more refrain, as if it were
the thread in the labyrinth that could save you.

REPRIEVE

If, as Rumi once wrote, *The price*
of kissing is my life: at least

this morning, let me not think
about all that there is too

much of—the weight of living
accrued in collapsible boxes,

all the kisses that have morphed
into deeds and contracts, the kisses

now overlaid with the smell of musty
evenings in old countries, those

that smack of the toil that comes
of trying to sweeten others' days—

Surely there is room for some plain,
no-strings-attached kissing, surely

a way to modulate the hum of that one
cicada in the trees so its voice lifts,

doesn't merely drown, in a chorus of other
insistent voices? Surely there must be a way

to lengthen the echoes of light sifting
in the leaves and through damp lattices

of neighbors' fences; to dwell without
rancor or remorse in moments when I

might press my face against your nape
to catch that drifting note—

unnameable, unmistakable, stirring
even my sorrows into fragrance.

HALLUCINATORIO

after Roberto Bolaño's "A Stroll Through Literature"

1. I dream of blood that wells from a cut, uncoils its wavelengths of sequestered light, turns more solid than the furniture in my house.

2. In my dream it is Lent, just like it is right now. *Guardia civil* are herding *babaylanes* into yellow Humvees. Their bandannas, knotted under the chin, catch the glow of sunset. The vehicles rev up and head toward the hills. When the dust settles, the townsfolk find they cannot erase the ancient writing that has formed beneath tire tracks. It becomes their new epic poem. They will read it every year. Movie producers will come to film it.

3. In my dream it is still Lent. Which can mean any of a number of things: penitents stripped to the waist, their heads wrapped in sack-cloth, their brows circled with crude vines or barbed wire. Their backs: red labyrinths, ladders gorged with flame.

4. In another dream all the lilies have open vestments. The children come to gather pollen in their cups. Every eyelid will be streaked with gold, every finger outlined with knowing.

5. I dream that in the ruined chapel, above carpets of moss, a cherub ziplines toward me from the belfry. *When was the last time you washed your face?* I ask my soul. It likes to play in the mud, where it is cool. It hangs its head to one side; it doesn't like to brush its hair.

6. *Donde? Aqui, aqui.*

7. In this dream, I knock on the door of room after room until I come to the one where *Prinsipe* Florante is lashed to a tree, bemoaning his fate. If I turn the right combination of locks hidden in the leaves, we will understand each other perfectly, in monorhyming quatrains filled with lyric and metaphor. And the lion will slink back into the darkness from which it came.

8. In this dream I gently cover the woman's mouth with my hand, lead her into a room which has temporarily been stripped of all reminders of her sons; I bathe her fevered brow with water. If you lived her story, you too would be crazed. Later in the night,

the oil lamp that should have ignited the revolution the first time, will burn down the governor's house.

9. In this dream it is many years since you have touched me. By this I mean the premises have fallen silent. Sometimes it is not a dream.

10. The poet leaves: she is outcast from her hometown. Does she drink? Chew betel nut leaf? Swear like a *cargador* at the pier? Gamble away her children's inheritance? Smoke cigars with the lit end in her mouth? Take lovers, including her maid? Wear only pants? Burn her bra? You have no imagination if you think this is all it takes to be a poet.

ACKNOWLEDGMENTS

"Appetite" appeared in *Tongue Journal,* Winter 2013.

"Hallucinatorio" appeared in a Curated Prompt in *Lantern Review:* Poetry as Speculum, Luisa A. Igloria http://www.lanternreview.com/blog/2012/05/11/curated-prompt-luisa-a-igloria-poetry-as-speculum/.

"Reprieve" appears as a videopoem collaboration (poetry by Luisa A. Igloria, video poem/film poem by Dave Bonta) at http://vimeo.com/28563595 and at http://www.youtube.com/watch?v=x5N5tp4gtAw.

Many of the poems in this manuscript were first written and posted online at Dave Bonta's *Via Negativa* site (they are archived at http://www.vianegativa.us/author/luisa/) as part of Luisa A. Igloria's daily poem writing practice. She has written at least a poem a day since 20 November 2010.

ABOUT THE AUTHOR

A well-published poet, Luisa A. Igloria is professor of creative writing and English, and director of the MFA creative writing program at Old Dominion University. Beyond the thirteen books she has previously published, her work has appeared in numerous anthologies and journals including *Poetry, Crab Orchard Review, The Missouri Review, Indiana Review, Poetry East, Umbrella, Sweet, qarrtsiluni, poemeleon, Smartish Pace, Rattle, The North American Review, Bellingham Review, Shearsman* (UK), *PRISM International* (Canada), *Poetry Salzburg Review* (Austria), *The Asian Pacific American Journal,* and *TriQuarterly.* Since November 2010, she has written at least a poem a day; these poems are archived at http://www.vianegativa.us. Originally from Baguio City in the Philippines, Igloria has four daughters and now makes her home in Virginia with most of her family.

THE MAY SWENSON POETRY AWARD

The May Swenson Poetry Award, an annual competition named for May Swenson, honors her as one of America's most provocative and vital writers. During her long career, Swenson was loved and praised by writers from virtually every school of American poetry. Winner of a MacArthur, a Guggenheim, and many other awards, she left a legacy of fifty years of writing when she died in 1989. She is buried in Logan, Utah, her hometown.